Gina

America's Ultimate Reminders® Coach

Thriving at Work

- Make Your Mark
- Lead With Confidence
- Stomp Out Drama
- Get Home by 6:00

Ultimate Reminders, LLC
8895 Towne Centre Dr. Suite 105-210
San Diego, CA 92122
UltimateReminders.com

The anecdotes and advice herein are not intended to replace the services of trained mental health professionals. You are advised to consult with your healthcare professional with regard to matters relating to your mental health, and in particular, regarding matters that may require diagnosis or medical attention. The author and publisher specifically disclaim any liability that is incurred from the use or application of the contents of this book.

The names and identifying characteristics of some of the individuals featured throughout this book have been changed to protect their privacy. Any resemblance to actual persons, living or dead, is purely coincidental.

Book Design by GKS Creative

First edition

Library of Congress Control Number: 2017918757

ISBN: 978-0-9896291-9-5

For employers and employees everywhere—
to inspire you to thrive and remind you how to do it.

Also by Gina DeLapa

Thriving at Work (audiobook)
Ultimate Reminders for Everyday Life
Ultimate Reminders for College Students

Contents

Note to the Reader: Why *Thriving at Work*?

As an adult, you will probably spend more time working than you spend on any other waking activity. For that reason alone, not to mention the many layers of meaning contained in your life's work, you deserve to make your work more meaningful, productive, fulfilling, and fun.

In case it needs to be said, your work also needs to be *sustainable.* As an example, recently one of my fellow public speakers reported he had been averaging three to four hours' sleep each night for months.

That's a recipe for burnout.

Enter *Thriving at Work.* I wrote this book to help you go from ever burning out to always breaking through. The career counselor in me knows when work goes well, life goes well. And when work goes poorly, satisfactions outside of work rarely if ever compensate.

But what if you could go to work each day feeling recharged, refreshed, respected, and appreciated? Imagine if these attributes permeated your entire workplace.

Thriving at Work will help you create that culture, one fulfilled employee at a time. Let the transformation begin with you!

To help you succeed, you will find a mix of serious and playful, humorous and poignant. You will also have the chance to visit and revisit some of my most requested stories.

A sneak peek at the four themes of *Thriving at Work*:

Taking Care of YOU, Guilt-Free

While other books focus on how to create a thriving culture, experience tells me that the effort has to begin inside the hearts and minds of individual employees.

When employees are on board, in word and deed, company-wide investments catch on much more quickly and yield much higher returns.

Not to mention that everywhere I go and everywhere I speak, employees at all levels are hungry for this message. Few of us are suffering from too much self-care.

In fact, I have never met a professional man or woman whose performance suffered because they placed top priority on their physical, mental, emotional, and spiritual well-being.

Yet I've known countless professionals who, having ignored their own needs, sentenced themselves, their work, and their relationships to a lifetime of regret and lost fulfillment.

It just doesn't have to be that way.

Within this section, you will find the tools and inspiration to make self-care an ongoing top priority.

Each reflection is short enough to digest and in-depth enough to make a practical difference.

Leadership, Etiquette & Professionalism

My first lesson in leadership, etiquette and professionalism came when my boss's boss told me politely to stop saying "Yeah." I was ten years old.

Working in my parents' frozen foods business gave me an early exposure to what management expected from employees and what employees needed in return to feel valued and fulfilled.

That perspective, both as an employer and an employee, has never left me. On the contrary, it has grown and developed from that day to this. It continues to inform both my writing and my public speaking.

My early exposure to the American professional workplace also helped drive my decision to move to California in 2001 to pursue a master's degree in counseling with an emphasis in career development.

I owe a debt of gratitude to the University of San Diego for making that degree possible, along with nearly every contribution I've made since then—from serving as a university career counselor to returning to my alma mater as an adjunct faculty member to teaching workplace etiquette to new college hires on Wall Street to bringing you this book.

Within this section, you will find what you need to be at your professional best—whether you serve in a formal leadership role or not. My own feeling is that leadership is a mindset, not a particular role or title.

Stomping Out Drama

Show me a workplace that hasn't had drama, and I'll show you a consultant who doesn't want to change your logo.

What matters is not whether your workplace has drama, but how well you handle it and what you're willing to do to put drama in its place.

This is the shortest section of the book, and I think that says something about my philosophy on drama: Deal with it head on, and be done with it.

Chapters such as "The Weapons That Defeat Drama" drive home this point. Be fair yet firm, and do not let drama eat your organization alive. Life is too short, and the competition is too fierce.

How to Make Your Mark

As with the previous sections, "How to Make Your Mark" could comprise an entire book. But the goal here is to spark meaningful action, not to write a treatise.

Incidentally, I once picked up a 300-page book called *Focus.* I decided if I simply followed that one word of advice, I would be infinitely better off than if I had read all 300 pages and done nothing different. I gave the book away and never looked back.

This section reminds you that opportunities for meaning and fulfillment are all around you. And you already *are* making your mark.

May you be inspired to reach even higher and make more of a difference than you can possibly imagine. The question posed in the chapter "Learning to Say Goodbye" says it all:

How would you like to be remembered?

Gina DeLapa
America's Ultimate Reminders® Coach
San Diego, California

PART 1:

Taking Care of YOU, Guilt-Free

"You will never feel truly satisfied by work until you are satisfied by life."

—HEATHER SCHUCK,
The Working Mom Manifesto

Why Self-Care Isn't Selfish

When you were in school, did you ever learn something that had nothing to do with a textbook?

Imagine you're a first-year college student, as I was, and it's coming near the end of fall term. Like most (clueless) freshmen, I'm having a blast.

So much so that I barely notice how much I'm struggling in three of my classes.

The one exception is Latin. Second-Year Latin—I am a beast. What Merle Haggard is to music, what Fabio is to hair, I am to the Latin language.

And it doesn't hurt that my professor—a nice guy not too much older than I am—is kind of cute. (I'm Catholic, not blind.) He's like Prince William in tweed and tennis shoes.

Fast-forward to the beginning of finals week. I'm up late at night, studying my little heart out. And I'm not too concerned about the Latin final, even though it's the next morning. I'm much more concerned with classes two, three, and four.

Finally, my eyes can't take it anymore. So I shut the books, set my alarm, and curl up nice and tight in my J.C. Penney powder-blue twin comforter. My head hits the pillow and before I know it I pop awake, ready to go crush that Latin final.

Then I look up at the clock and realize *I SLEPT THROUGH IT!* By several hours.

I blew it. How do you tell someone you blew it? I'll tell you how (no rhyme intended): You just do it. This is in my book *Ultimate Reminders for Everyday Life*: When you mess up, fess up.

What happens to credibility when we own our mistakes? Does it go down or does it go up? That's right. It goes up. In my case, barely.

So I call the Classics Department in a panic. The office secretary answers and says the professor's not there. *Ugh.*

"But," she says, "he's left you a little note." Here's basically what the note said:

I'm going to let you still take the exam. But I'm going to make it harder. And I'm taking one letter off your exam grade right from the start. See you at two o'clock.

So I go in and take the exam, and roughly two weeks later my report card comes. And in that course where I should have had my only A, I got a stinkin' B.

By the way, did you know you can't get by on forty-five minutes' sleep? I do now.

But for what it's worth, I never again slept through a Latin final—or any other. I've spoken all over the country, and no matter what the time zone, I always make a point of showing up at least one hour early.

Never mind how many alarms I set.

Here in San Diego, I've had the privilege of appearing on FOX5 Morning News more than fifty times and counting. No matter what hour they want me there, I show up early.

So I know people can change—because I did. But what that exam experience taught me, you won't find on any transcript; namely, that in the great school called Life, taking care of yourself—physically, mentally, emotionally, and spiritually—is not an elective, is it?

No. It's a core requirement. And I've since boiled that down to the following. If you're taking notes, this would be an excellent note to make:

Self-care is oxygen.

That's how important it is. And like oxygen, you can't put it off until next week or next year. And you can't put it off on someone else's shoulders. There's no app for self-care. You just have to do it.

If you don't believe me, stop what you're doing and take two deep breaths.

How did that feel? I'm guessing during those two breaths you did not feel one ounce of guilt. Am I right?

Yet you may have somehow convinced yourself that self-care is "selfish." On the contrary, self-care is your only shot at breathing more life into everything you do—from keeping your commitments to enjoying healthy relationships to finding fulfillment every single day.

I invite you to read and sign the pledge on the next page, and keep it where you can refer to it daily. For a free 8 ½ x 11 copy of the pledge, which you can hang in your workspace or display on your refrigerator, visit ultimatereminders.com/free-downloads.

Take the Self-Care Pledge

I, ____,

pledge to make my own physical, mental, emotional, and spiritual self-care a top priority.

I do so not at the expense of my other commitments, but at their service. I trust that the relationships that are right for me will grow stronger when I keep this pledge.

By honoring my limitations, saying no when necessary, and doing what it takes to stay healthy in every sense of the word, I set a powerful example for those around me, thus helping create a world and workplace where every person can thrive, including me!

______________________________ ______________

Name Today's Date

The Best Decisions Start with These Five Words

If your dad is anything like my dad, he is most hilarious when he is not trying to be. Case in point: the Las Vegas commute "Kick it in the ass!" story.[1]

The five words I started to tell you about may not be as humorous as "Kick it in the ass!" But (no pun intended) you may find them more helpful:

Set yourself up for success.

Boom. A few examples of what it looks like to set yourself up for success:

- Not baking cookies when you've got one foot out the door to the airport (I know someone who used to do this)
- Building in a day or more *after* the vacation to ease back into your routine
- Saying no when it serves a more important "yes"

1 You'll find it in my first book, *Ultimate Reminders for Everyday Life*; specifically, in the Note to the Reader.

Setting yourself up for success applies to everything from what you eat for breakfast to how you prepare a speech to how you plan for retirement.

In fact, the more you apply these words throughout your day, the easier you will find it to make wise decisions and lower your stress for a lifetime.

What could you do, starting today, to set yourself up for success?

No Substitute for a Good Night's Rest

"If physical energy is the foundation of all dimensions of energy, sleep is the foundation of physical energy."
—TONY SCHWARTZ,
The Way We're Working Isn't Working

The next time you're tempted to cut out sleep, consider this: Sleep deprivation not only affects your mood and your immune system, ultimately it can take your life.

Here's the ultimate irony: Even with that said, sleep is often the first thing we sacrifice when it should be the first thing we safeguard.

Sleep deprivation is known to make you more irritable and more reactive. I don't know about you, but I don't need any help becoming irritable or more reactive.

Lack of sleep makes it harder for you to manage your emotions. And finally, it impairs your performance and judgment.

Whether you realize it or not, sleep deprivation also affects every relationship you have, every thought you have, and the quality of those thoughts.

Who *doesn't* feel better—more energized and almost invincible—after a good night's rest?

To help you sleep better starting tonight, I teamed up with my friend Jeff Scheuer, who has earned the title America's Beducator.™ You can find his videos on YouTube and more about him on his website, matt-to-go.com.

11 Tips for Better Sleep

1. **Limit use of electronic devices one to two hours before bed.** Electronic devices stimulate the brain, which needs a chance to shut off and time to ramp down.
2. **Allow your entire body time to ramp down.** Starting one to two hours before bed, limit your

activity. (Gina's note: Try also dimming the lights and putting on some mellow music.)

3. **Avoid eating and drinking close to bedtime.** At least six hours before bed, stop drinking beverages with caffeine.
4. **Create a clean, healthy sleep environment.** Make sure your body is clean as well as your sheets. A warm bath or shower is a great way to relax and wind down before bed.
5. **Keep a notepad on your nightstand.** Writing things down helps turn off your brain. Trying to remember details of your day doesn't give the brain the time it needs to relax.
6. **Create a dark sleep environment.** Keep the shades drawn to minimize your exposure to light. Even with your eyes closed, you can still perceive light—and this could make it harder to get the deep, restorative sleep you need.
7. **Naps are not a four-letter word.** Take a 15- to 30-minute nap to recharge and reset. Avoid long naps, which can disrupt your sleep cycle.
8. **Control your bedroom's microclimate.** Keep

the air in the mid-to-upper 60s or low 70s and try to control humidity. According to the National Sleep Foundation, the ideal humidity range is from 30 to 50 percent.

9. **Don't turn your bedroom into an office.** You need to associate the bedroom with slumber. If it's used as an office, the brain gets reactivated.
10. **Keep your sleep schedule constant.** Even on weekends, stay within an hour or so of your normal wake-up time. When your sleep schedule is off, it can take days to reset it. The more you stick to a consistent sleep schedule, the more refreshed you will be in the morning.
11. **Don't hit the snooze button!** You won't wake up more rested. In fact, you will only feel worse. Challenge yourself to get up and stay up. Believe it or not, you will feel better!

Sleeping is the most important thing you can do, not only for restoration but for your short-term and long-term health. Good restoration correlates directly to better health, weight loss, and prevention of heart disease. With a few simple habits, you can overcome sleep deprivation and the health hazards that go with it.

P.S. The most important, most used piece of furniture you have is your mattress. How well is yours setting you up for optimal health?

Source: Jeff Scheuer, America's Beducator™ and owner of Mattress to Go (matt-to-go.com).

Lessons from My Friday-Morning Meltdown

Ever have a day where anything that could go wrong does? For me one Friday morning, it was discovering on my way out the door that a crucial email sent earlier in the week to my new attorney had never actually gone out—when it did, it was the wrong draft with the wrong attachments.

Lawyers love that.

Scrambling to find the right attachments before bolting out the door. Then getting caught in traffic on my way to an appointment. Parking drama.

The thrill of sliding into a new doctor's office with two minutes to spare, only to be handed a clipboard with a mountain of paperwork and a ballpoint pen.

More delays than I could count. Then being emotionally blindsided by the doctor I waited several weeks to see. *Just fix my arm, Bob.* To his credit, he did. But this would come later.

I once heard a comedian say God didn't give Californians rain because He knew they couldn't deal with it emotionally. The morning of my meltdown, there was no rain—only off-the-charts heat and humidity.

Now I realize that's a high-class problem. But that morning it was one more thing than I could take.

Thankfully, the frustration didn't last forever—and what it taught me just might help you manage your own frustration. But unlike me, you won't have to learn these lessons in hindsight.

Ultimate Reminder #1: Time-outs aren't just for toddlers.

When you're having a mini-breakdown, the best [illegible]ng you can do is acknowledge it. The sooner, the [illegible]r.

Think how much more peaceful our homes would be, how much workplace conflict could be nipped in the bud with one simple, matter-of-fact sentence: "I need a time-out."

Boom. Problem half solved. So how do you know when you need a time-out?

- Nothing is going right—including your ability to deal with it.
- You're using words you normally cringe at when you hear them spoken by others.
- You can't remember the last time you took a deep breath.

Ultimate Reminder #2: Stop and take a breath.

Maybe three. If you find this hard to do, all the more reason to do it. Taking a breath forces you to stop, regroup, and regain your perspective.

Ultimate Reminder #3: Ask yourself what you need.

Sometimes you won't know. Keep asking anyway. Start with the physical: Do you need sleep? Food? Water? Chocolate?

When the pressure's on, a friend of mine jokes about needing to get herself to a Mountain Dew. For me, it's a frozen treat from Trader Joe's called (ironically enough) "GONE BANANAS!"

When the stress piles on, what's your go-to, food-wise or otherwise?

Sometimes you just need to clean off your desk or take out the trash. Clearing mental hurdles, no matter how trivial they might seem to someone else, can restore hope and a healthy sense of order—and clarity.

Ultimate Reminder #4: Learn the lesson.

Whenever I go back to Michigan, I always notice and appreciate the living-room-size parking spots.

Here in Southern California, parking spots are about as wide as a Band-Aid. Michigan has bacon strips that are more generous.

As I learned again that Friday, California parking *garages* are even more drum tight. So next time I will find a way to park on the street. Or who knows? Maybe rent a Prius for the occasion.

The point is, I've made the executive decision to steer clear of parking garages. That decision was a real gift.

What lesson or decision would make *your* life easier?

Ultimate Reminder #5: Find the humor.

Have you ever had someone pierce you with a question you just weren't expecting? In my case it was that doctor I mentioned, the one I had just met.

He wasn't a bad guy. But after a few pleasantries, he launched right in with rumors going around the neighborhood—rumors about someone close to me, rumors that were ripping my heart out.

Then he asked if the rumors were true. *Are you taking bets*? I said I'm not at liberty to comment—which was true. *Dude, who taught you bedside manner*?!

Later when I shared this story with my niece, including the part about wanting to say "Just fix my arm (Bob)," it gave us both a good laugh.

Maybe that's the gift of losing our cool now and then: It allows us to stop, regroup, overcome, and ultimately laugh with those we love most.

The Key to Getting Yourself Unstuck

Have you ever felt stuck in a rut? Maybe in a project, a relationship, or your life in general?

An older, wiser massage therapist named Sally gave me the key to getting *un*stuck—in any area of life. The only time this key doesn't work is when you forget to use it.

One late afternoon, right in the middle of a massage, Sally asked me, "What does Gina need?" *Huh? Gina needs you to stop talking like Mister Rogers.*

I barely gave the question a second thought. Until one morning a few weeks later, when I stubbed my big toe on my way to the shower. Which is always fun.

Ever find yourself overreacting without knowing why?

Even as I pounded the wall and continued to curse, I knew something else was bothering me besides the smashed toe.

That night, I sat down at the kitchen table with a pen and pad of paper. And for the first time, I let Sally's question sink in. What *does* Gina need?

A brief list of what came out:

- Change of scenery
- Better weather
- A new career
- Something to write about besides 401(k) plans

Who knew? Then just like that, mental clarity morphed into overwhelming uncertainty. *What does this mean? Where would I go? What would I study? And what would I do with my house? My business?*

I spent the next six months soul-searching, reading books, listening to audio programs, conducting informational interviews, praying the biggest prayers I knew how, and chasing a lot of dead ends.

For example, I had sent away for a graduate catalog from the University of San Diego. But by the time it showed up in my mailbox, I had already crossed off the program that sparked my interest in the first place.

But I couldn't help notice that the USD catalog cover was total eye candy. To a Midwesterner like me, a campus with palm trees and a view of the ocean was almost more than I could hope for.

Almost.

It turns out USD offered a graduate program in counseling with an emphasis in career development. *I was made for this.* No particular undergraduate major required, no GRE. *Yay.*

Someone close to me kept asking, "What if you don't get in?"

What if I do and it turns out to be the best thing since Trader Joe's peanut butter?

Not only did I get in, I went on to be named Outstanding Student of the Year within the career specialization. More importantly, I landed my dream job before graduation.

As an editor and copywriter, I was tired of always interviewing experts. I wanted to become one. I did. Soon after beginning my full-time job as a university career counselor, I was asked to write a career column called "Senior Year" for a Dow Jones website.

All of this started when I asked myself that simple question posed by my friend Sally: "What does Gina need?"

Try it. Ask yourself right out loud, "What does (your name) need?" Your answers will help you get unstuck. What you do with those answers just might change your world.

"What Does (Your Name) Need?"*

Take out a sheet of paper, and across the top write "What Does (Your Name) Need?"

Underneath, brainstorm a list of what you need to thrive at work. Don't analyze as you go. Just let the thoughts pour.

When you've listed up to twenty items, place a star next to one that you could make time for in the coming week. Maybe it's a walk after dinner. Maybe it's laughing with an old friend.

Whatever it is, block some time on your calendar to make it happen. Jot down how you feel afterward. Better yet, if you want your life to never be the same, schedule your non-negotiable needs on a regular basis.

* *To download a free worksheet for this exercise, visit ultimatereminders.com/free-downloads.*

9 Reasons Not to Be a People-Pleaser

Have you ever had one of those lightbulb moments that stays with you for a lifetime? When I was in my twenties, I heard a speaker named Nancy Skinner say, "A strength overused is a weakness." *Boom.*

Those six little words sum up the problem with people-pleasing. It turns out that paying too much attention to what others think can do more harm than good—not only to you, but to the person you're trying to please.

1. Pleasing everyone is impossible. And what would you gain if you did?
2. It's exhausting. I once heard Dr. Bernie Siegel say with all warmth and sincerity, "When you learn to say no, illness doesn't need to say it for you." *Ow.* But there's some truth to that.
3. Anyone who does expect you to cater to their every whim is probably not someone who adds

joy to your life. At the very least, the relationship may need fine-tuning.

4. Joy is part of the deal. You were made for joy. Excessive people-pleasing drains joy.

5. You can get so good at pleasing other people that you expect them to do the same for you. If only it worked that way. To quote Jim Rohn, "I'll take care of me for you, if you will please take care of you for me."

6. The people who are right for you don't want you to be a people-pleaser. It's draining for them too. They love, like, and respect you for you—not what you can do for them.

7. Trying to please everyone turns out to be unfair. Why? Because it hurts the people you love the most and shortchanges the projects that matter most. Put your time and energy where it counts, and notice how your whole life improves.

8. Pleasing other people can be surprisingly self-serving. Ever been around someone whose need to be needed was greater than your need? That, too, is exhausting—and just not necessary.

9. You are setting an example for those around you—especially those you love and work with. Make your example warm, sustainable, and fun.

Make your example one you enjoy living.

Take Charge of Your Finances

If you're going to thrive at work, you've got to get a handle on your finances: earning, spending, saving, investing, paying down debt, and planning for retirement.

Financial stress has a way of eating us up inside and spilling over into every area of life—including work, where we spend the bulk of our day. A former banker I know used to say that people would sooner divulge their mental illnesses than share their struggles with money.

More recently, psychologists have coined the term Acute Financial Stress (AFS). It is far more common than you might think.

According to a 2015 survey involving a random sample of 2,041 Americans, nearly one out of four Americans—and more than a third of millennials—experience a debilitating degree of stress surrounding their finances.

Why wait until you're in that state to get help? And if you're already there, rest assured there's help and hope.

Though it goes beyond the scope of this book, here are a few basic principles to ease financial stress:

Reach out for help as soon as possible. The sooner you reach out, the greater your options and flexibility. Not sure where to start? Try GerriDetweiler.com.

Gerri and I worked together when I was the editor of two personal-finance newsletters. Her site offers helpful, trustworthy tips along with resources for saving money, repairing credit, and much more.

Take full advantage of any employer match. It's tax-deferred income. If you're not contributing enough to your 401(k), 403(b), or IRA to reap the full match, you're leaving money on the table—money that could be accumulating on your behalf, even while you sleep.

Make sure you're investing aggressively enough for retirement. Many people play it too safe. Check with your employer to seek out financial guidance for your specific circumstances.

Do your best not to touch your retirement funds before retirement. Your withdrawals will be taxed as ordinary income. What's worse, you will miss out on all that tax-deferred compound growth. Depending on your age, your withdrawals may also be subject to a 10% penalty.

Careful when you change employers. If you're moving your retirement funds to a new plan, be sure to do what's known as a direct rollover, direct transfer, or trustee-to-trustee transfer. This is a seamless process for moving your funds while allowing them to continue enjoying tax-deferred status—free of penalty.

Beware the temptation to micromanage. Who likes to be micromanaged? No one. The same is true for your investments. Choose the best investments you can for your circumstances and give them time to perform. A good financial advisor can help you stay calm and make wise decisions, even through the market's inevitable ups and downs.

Talk about it. When you're struggling financially, one of the worst things you can do is try to handle it all on your own. You might feel more comfortable starting the conversation with someone you know will be safe—for example, a counselor, clergy member, or close friend.

Tough as it might be, enlist the support of your loved ones (e.g., spouse and children). Even if the discussions are heated, stay the course. In time, those discussions are likely to cool off and give way to financial solutions.

P.S. When you feel as though you're struggling financially, giving to charity might be the last thing on your mind. But I would encourage you not to miss out on the joy and benefits of generosity.

For the free article "Generosity on Any Income," visit UltimateReminders.com/free-downloads.

your "no" poorly. And guess what? That's
ust let them own their response. Your job is
itely hold your ground. Incidentally, people
poor boundaries will always find it difficult
nor yours. Honor your boundaries anyway.

yes to what counts. Whether it's pouring
rself into your work, your family, your
ication, or anything else, it's always easier to
no when you've figured out your bigger yes.

Say No with a Smile, Say Yes to What Matters

If you want your life to be less stressful and more fulfilling, you're going to have to say no to a lot of opportunities, even good ones. Your reward? More time for the contributions you were meant to make, the ones that light you up.

How I learned to say no with a smile

Someone once asked me to take over a volunteer newsletter, when my full-time job was overseeing two newsletters. By the sheer grace of God, I heard myself say nice as pie, "I need to let that opportunity go to someone else."

Bingo. It was true! I had to turn down the volunteer role so I could give myself fully to the professional role—and not burn out. What about you?

Which of your roles need nurturing and protecting?

For example, maybe you're the family breadwinner—

or the parent of teenagers who will be soon be heading off to college. Or a proud grandparent. These are roles worth protecting, even if it means saying no to other non-work priorities.

For myself, I want to take time to enjoy visits with my parents. I want to spend less time filing papers and more time creating. Right now, I'm creating this book and a couple of speeches, which really do light me up.

What lights you up?

Or to put it more simply, what's at the top of your priority list? How will these priorities be affected by new requests? Once you reflect on your answers, it becomes easier to say yes with conviction or no with a smile.

5 Ways Easier

1. **Check your neck.** If t even to something goo neck (or your gut), that c of saying, "Don't do it." your body is telling you. If limitations, who will?
2. **Let the other person save fac** have to mean beating someone And of course, not all "no's" h line in the sand. For example, y alternative—or ask for a rain chec
3. **Don't give false hope.** If the reques really isn't up for debate, why give that it is? Find a way instead to gent door. For example, you can say, "I've ju much on my plate." No explanations, feelings.
4. **Let others own their drama.** No matter ho and diplomatic you are, some people are goi

react to okay! to pol with to ho

5. **Say** you edu say

What's Draining Your Battery?

When you ask yourself "What's draining my battery?" be prepared for the avalanche of answers—but don't be disheartened. Though the length of your list might surprise you, so will the simplicity of your solutions.

In my case, I had thought all my recent energy drain was coming from one place. Instead, what poured out was a list of items numbering more than fifteen: everything from lack of consistent sleep to feeling behind on key projects.

Ultimate Reminder #1: Dare to name what's draining you. Only then can you do something constructive about it.

I saw that most of the items on my list had a few common threads: procrastination, indecision, and good old-fashioned clutter.

Without much forethought, I picked up the last item on my list (deciding whether to have my upcoming speech professionally videotaped), set a timer for eight minutes, and just dealt with it.

It took closer to fifteen minutes and a flurry of messages with the newly hired videographer. But I now had one less energy leak—and one more reason to knock this speech out of the park.

Where is indecision costing you time and energy? What would happen if you took time today to deal with it?

Emboldened by having cleared one hurdle, I conquered another—one that fell under the category of *clutter.*

Specifically, I removed myself from a handful of mailing lists; the ones that weren't adding value to my life. In the words of James Veitch, "The Internet gave us access to everything. But it also gave everything access to us."

Ultimate Reminder #2:
Let yourself turn the corner.

As I looked over my shrinking list of energy drains, my eyes fell on the one big item I alluded to earlier—and I finally accepted that it wasn't going to change.

So with a new season on the horizon, I made the executive decision to let it go. I can't tell you what a relief this was, how much lighter I felt afterward.

A few hours later, I noticed my hand, wrist, and forearm, which had been bothering me all summer, felt surprisingly pain-free.

I asked my acupuncturist, "Is that normal?" She smiled and said, "I see it all day long."

What is it time for you to leave behind? Why not give yourself that gift?

PART 2: Leadership, Etiquette & Professionalism

"Great leaders don't need to act tough. Their confidence and humility serve to underscore their toughness."

—SIMON SINEK

The 7 Cs of Effective Leadership

If you're a leader in the formal sense, how would your team rate you on the following seven qualities?

Character. Can you be counted on to do the right thing, even when no one else is looking? Do you make decisions based not on what's popular but on what's best for the organization?

Competence. Billy Joel said, "I've reached the age where competence is a turn-on." When you don't know something, how willing are you to ask questions and listen? To learn new skills?

Courage. Are you willing to confront and be confronted? To lead by word and example, so your entire team can thrive? To admit when you were wrong and make restitution?

Confidence. Are you willing to set the bar high for your team, both in performance and conduct? Does your team feel supported?

Communication. Are you appropriately forthright with your team? Does your communication style leave others feeling confident in your leadership?

Class. Are senior managers and janitors equally comfortable in your presence? Do you go out of your way to help others feel included, valued, heard, and respected?

Credibility. If you master the first six Cs, your credibility is all but guaranteed. In fact, it will come through crystal clear in everything you do.

Cultivating these characteristics can take a lifetime—and not all embrace the opportunity. But when you do, you discover a joy in what you have chosen to become. You discover a joy that nothing and no one can take from you.

How to Be a Better Listener (and Why)

Is there any higher form of respect than listening? If you want to gain respect as a world-class leader, you must first *give* respect by being a world-class listener.

9 Tips to Be a Better Listener

1. **Give your full attention** to the person speaking. For example, silence your phone, tone down the music, make eye contact, and don't let outside parties interrupt. Giving your full attention builds trust and saves time.

2. **Set aside what you're planning to say**. Focus instead on understanding the other person's message, both verbal and nonverbal. Remember that understanding doesn't necessarily mean agreement.

3. **Check for understanding**. It helps if you can do this non-judgmentally. "So if I'm hearing

you correctly" comes across more palatably than "So what you're saying is . . ."

4. **Acknowledge**. For example, if someone's venting, chances are they don't want you to solve their problem—they just want to feel heard and understood.

5. **Let the other person talk!** Even too many words of agreement (e.g., "Right, right") can be disruptive—they may even signify impatience or tuning out.

6. **Use open, friendly posture and facial gestures** to show you're receptive and tuning in.

7. **Don't be afraid to pause before responding**, particularly when the stakes are high.

8. **Take notes**. This is especially important when someone is sharing dates, deadlines, or other details of an important project.

9. **Summarize key details** (e.g., phone numbers, dates) so the other person knows you're clear on what's just been said.

Finally, be willing to listen even when it's uncomfortable. Be willing to take the action that is yours to take—without delay, without excuses. It probably *will* be uncomfortable. But your integrity as a leader demands no less.

No More Mindless Meetings

Running effective meetings isn't hard—it just takes caring and competence, planning and practice. Your reward will be more time for the work that matters most, and meetings that boost productivity.

The 7 Must-Haves of Meetings

1. **A purpose that passes the snow-day test.** Imagine on the day of your meeting, a snowstorm keeps all of you homebound. Could you accomplish the meeting's mission in some other way (e.g., conference call, email)? Could you get by without rescheduling? If the answer to either of those questions is "Yes," consider switching to a Plan B.

2. **A designated leader.** Every effective meeting needs someone to lead from start to finish, and to walk the line between allowing others to be heard, and staying on topic. A good leader sets a positive, energetic tone while making optimum use of the group's time.

3. **A clear goal, or set of goals.** What needs to be accomplished? What's at stake? Who needs to attend, and who simply needs to be kept informed? Consider using a meeting-cost calculator to gain further insight into who needs to attend and how long the meeting should last. Why have thousand-dollar meetings to make ten-dollar decisions?

4. **A carefully chosen environment.** The ideal environment suits the meeting's purpose, is accessible and well lit, has the required audio-visual equipment, and is comfortable, without inviting naps! *Subliminal message: No beanbag chairs.*

5. **A clear agenda, sent in advance.** If you're leading, allow time for participants to send you any changes, so you can send a final agenda before the meeting. Taking these steps shows respect for others' time and contribution—while letting participants know how they should prepare. Your agenda should specify the meeting location, start and end times, objectives, who's expected to attend, and who's accountable for each agenda item.

6. **Ground rules.** Will you start the meeting on time, even if someone is late? Does the group

know where you stand on the use of cell phones? How about other electronic devices? Do you have standards in place for how participants are to treat one another? Identifying and upholding even a few simple ground rules will help keep your meetings focused and constructive.

7. **A designated note-taker.** Have someone on your team track who's in attendance, key outcomes, decisions made, next steps (including who's responsible), and so on. Meeting minutes help keep the group informed and accountable—and if you ever need documentation for more serious matters (e.g., performance issues), detailed minutes can be a lifesaver.

Honesty vs. Integrity

Integrity includes honesty but goes far beyond it. Integrity also requires attributes such as benevolence and good judgment for its completion. A few examples:

Lacking Integrity	Showing Integrity
Criticizing with no regard for how the criticism will be received	Addressing behavior; showing respect for the person while still holding him or her accountable
Placing the need to be liked (or to avoid tough decisions) above doing what is best for the organization	Acting in the organization's best interests; seeking outside support, if necessary
Letting direct reports hear news through the grapevine, instead of from the source	Sharing news that is yours to share; allowing others to do the same
Sidestepping an employee's poor performance, including poor attitude, at the expense of the team	Acknowledging the true cost of poor performance; addressing it fairly and directly
Ignoring a personal or professional flaw that undermines relationships and/or performance	Seeking out feedback, even before it becomes necessary
Not admitting or apologizing for mistakes	Owning up to faults and, if necessary, rebuilding trust

Ultimately, all of these examples—and the countless examples that spring up daily within your own organization—boil down to one simple question:

Do others trust in your integrity and ability to lead?

If not, what are you willing to do to improve? Therein lies integrity's ultimate test.

"Your Last Words Linger" (So Do Your First)

On my last trip to Vegas, at a conference for public speakers, a speech coach named Patricia Fripp uttered the memorable line, "*Your last words linger.*"

Her point: Choose your words carefully—and think about their impact. This is why I don't end correspondence with "Regards," "Best," or "Sent from my iPhone."

Call them pet peeves, but that last one in particular just sort of ruins it for me—mostly in a humorous way. As in, "I will love you till the end of time. Sent from my iPhone."

See what I mean? *Your last words linger.*

Personal musings aside, our first words also linger. Which is why when you hear the statements below, you might want to head for the hills—or at least detach a little. Incidentally, this list is funnier if you read it out loud.

15 Ways *Not* to Start a Conversation

I'll be honest.
I mean no disrespect.
No offense.
I'll play devil's advocate.
I'm sorry if.
Don't get me wrong.
I just assumed.
It's not my fault.
Quite frankly.
Why did you (fill in the blank)?
Bless your heart.
You look tired.
Did I wake you up?
Smile!
We need to talk.

On the positive side, words can also bring comfort, connection, understanding, and hope. Examples: *We'll make it work. I'll be there. Take your time. Consider it done.*

Words have power. Look for ways to use that power for good—and watch what it does not only for your relationships, but even more so for you.

The True Test of Any Apology

Does it restore trust?

Apologies that are insincere, incomplete, poorly delivered, and not backed up with a change in behavior—or better yet, a change of heart—can damage trust more than no apology at all. In the workplace, where achieving organizational goals hinges on trust and teamwork, effective apologies are not optional.

The higher your position, the more important this issue becomes. Why? Because you're standing in the spotlight, where your imperfections are much more visible, and where much more is expected of you.

More to the point, if you want to keep your best people, you need to give them an example worth following.

5 Keys to a Decent Apology

1. **When you mess up, fess up**. The ideal time to do this is before you have to. Let your respect for the other person come through in ways that can be felt. How? By going to the person directly and

owning up to your actions, without undue self-justification. Let your sincerity come through in your timing, your words, your voice, your body language, and facial cues.

2. **Acknowledge your impact, not just your intent**. Few of us go around intentionally hurting others. But that doesn't necessarily diminish our impact. If I step on your toe, even though I didn't mean to, it still hurts. If I repeatedly make the same offhand remark, it might erode your trust in me, even though I meant no harm. Be ready to acknowledge how your words and actions affect those around you—and change when necessary to restore the relationship. It's less about "correctness" and more about credibility.

3. **Let the other person know how things will be different**. But what about when things *won't* be different? For example, when someone wants more of your energy than you're feeling able or obligated to give. Or the employee who wants you to lower your standards for performance.

Even then, honor your boundaries while letting the other person save face.

4. **Stay focused on your goal**: namely, to work through the issue at hand in a way that restores trust and respect. This is not the time to turn the tables or bring up extraneous issues.

5. **Never think that saying "I'm sorry" makes you weak**. On the contrary, apologizing effectively takes tremendous strength, not to mention social grace. If you can rise to the occasion, your apologies will stand the best possible chance of being well received.

By owning up to your human frailty, and making it your job to overcome it, you will deepen trust across the organization, one relationship at a time.

And when you receive an apology? Accept it graciously. A sincere "Apology accepted" is often all you need to close the loop and get the relationship back on track.

What to Do with Negative Feedback

"Are you polishing my mirror or scratching it?"
—BERNIE SIEGEL, MD

I wish I could tell you that all the feedback you encounter will be delivered with compassion and class—unfortunately, we both know that just won't be the case.

So it helps to be able to discern the feedback that comes your way—and benefit from it as much as possible.

Ask yourself: Is the feedback a pattern or an isolated incident? If *one* person says something harsh, it may have more to do with that person. Let them own it.

But if you hear the same feedback from multiple sources, especially unrelated sources, it might be time to look in the mirror. Ask, "What can I learn from this?"

Sometimes the best response to feedback you might rather not hear is a simple "Thank you." If feedback helps you learn, grow, or improve, you've just received a gift. And if the feedback is unmerited, you've just received another lesson in maintaining healthy boundaries.

Remember that boundaries begin inside us. They are limits on what we will accept. Good internal boundaries remind us not to own words or behavior that don't belong to us.

Learn how to benefit from feedback—neither dismissing it outright nor letting it devastate you. This is one of the best ways to strengthen self-respect and respect from those around you. It is also a key ingredient for personal and professional growth.

4 Tests of Constructive Feedback

1. Is this the best time and place?
2. Am I the one who needs to bring this up?
3. Is the other person capable of hearing and benefiting from what I'm wanting to say?
4. Does it need mentioning at all?

Sometimes the answer is "No, but I need to say this anyway." In that case, don't be afraid to speak up.

But if the answer to these questions is just plain no, try biting your tongue. Better to put your energy where it will give you the best return on your investment.

Turning Fear Into Confidence

When you know defeat is not your destiny, it's easier to rise above life's inevitable setbacks—even when those setbacks involve your own public performance.

What is it time for you to stop being afraid of?

As an example, I figured out in tenth grade that I had a knack for public speaking—but it wasn't until I gave my best speech ever that I made the conscious decision to stop being afraid of public speaking.

Giving a speech is the fun part.

It's an incredible feeling to stand before an audience, get them involved, see them laugh and take notes, and watch the meeting planner's objectives come alive. And of course, mingle with the group afterward and sign books.

What's hard is all the work it takes to make a speech look effortless.

But like anything else challenging and worthwhile, once you accept the challenge and consciously commit, the work becomes less daunting. And with repeat practice, success starts to come more easily.

The same Ultimate Reminders that worked for me can work wonders for you as well—whether you're giving a speech, giving a toast, interviewing for a job, or taking on some other task where the stakes are high.

5 Ways to Turn Fear Into Confidence

1. **Start with a list.** What will success look like, and what are all the steps you'll need to get there? Getting it all out in front of you drives home the point that the list is finite. I would rather use a free app like Wunderlist than stare at my own (chicken-scratch) handwriting. It's also nice being able to move items around easily and share the list with others.

2. **Anticipate the obstacles.** For example, you don't want to get to a job interview and have to ask to borrow a pen—or apologize for not having extra

copies of your resume. Whenever I'm giving a presentation, I put all my slides and handouts on a thumb drive. I also email the files to myself, just in case. And you never go wrong by bringing your own water.

3. **Take more breaks.** Sometimes your brain just needs a rest. Use those times to prepare for your event in other ways—setting out your clothes, for example, or doing a drive-by of the location so you're not stressing out at the last minute. The day before that speech I mentioned, I filled the gas tank, got a car wash, *and* did a drive-by. All three helped me feel less nervous.

4. **Plan to show up early.** For a test or job interview, maybe ten minutes early. For a speech? Plan on a good hour. You'll need that time to settle in, set up the room, and handle any last-minute changes.

5. **Practice more than what seems necessary.** Don't worry about sounding "canned." More people fail for lack of preparation than for too much.

Finally, take good notes on what life teaches you—especially after an important event. This is one of the surest ways to reinforce good habits, turn snafus into success, and keep your confidence levels moving ever higher.

Interested in becoming a better public speaker? For the free report "Confidence, Credibility, and Results: How to Structure a Powerful Presentation," visit UltimateReminders.com/free-downloads.

10 Non-Negotiables of Every True Professional

My father says going to college taught him to say "That's incredible!" instead of "No sh*t!" We should all have been so lucky.

Here are ten more lessons you might not have learned in school, but will serve you throughout your career. If you're serious about gaining trust and credibility, these really aren't optional.

1. **Be neat and clean.** Nothing undermines professionalism like body odor, bedhead, or bad breath. You know this, of course. But not everyone does.

2. **Be punctual.** As the saying goes, "If you're early, you're on time. If you're on time, you're late. And if you're late, don't bother."

3. **Be prepared.** If you're going into a meeting, have everything you need from a pen and paper to key documents to a Kleenex. Be one step ahead. So many people go through life two steps behind.

4. **Smile and stand up straight.** Let your body language convey confidence. If you show confidence, you'll invite confidence.

5. **Have a sincere handshake.** This is another way to show professionalism and goodwill. A couple of smooth pumps and you're done.

6. **Make polite eye contact.** No up-and-down gaze, no peering into someone's soul, just a friendly, non-threatening eye-to-eye connection.

7. **Use positive, affirming language.** Skip the gossip, bad-mouthing, or trash-talk of any kind. Especially in front of clients or customers.

8. **Keep confidences.** At the same time, don't be someone's verbal dumping ground.

9. **Follow through.** Without being asked.

10. **Don't overshare.** No one needs to know you hang out at a nudist camp, make your own deodorant, or had a dream about the copy-machine repair guy. *I've heard all three.*

What else would you add to this list? What's one thing you can do, starting today, to model professionalism in the workplace?

A Few Words About Email

Whenever you send a workplace email, let your professionalism and regard for the human being(s) on the receiving end shine through. Toward *that* end . . .

1. Use an accurate, meaningful subject line.
2. Be brief. Respect your reader's time. Writing a short email might take longer than writing a long one. Send a short one anyway.
3. Clarify the precise action steps you would like your reader to take. Communicate those steps politely.
4. Communicate so clearly you can't be misunderstood. Phrases such as "client issues" could mean issues facing the client or issues you're having *with* the client. Be specific.
5. Speak in terms of the other person's time zone. *Example:* "I will call you at 8 am Pacific Time/11 am Eastern Time."
6. Keep it professional. Emojis, LOL, and "You

guys rock!" might work well for a class reunion, but not in the workplace. Likewise for opening with "Hey."

7. Use proper spelling and punctuation. And proofread. Don't say "asses" when you mean *assess* or "manger" when you mean *manager.*

8. If it's a high-stakes email, wait till you're done proofing before adding the recipient. It will save you from accidentally firing off a half-baked message. Along those lines, attach documents *before* sending your email, so they're not accidentally omitted.

9. Send and reply only to those who need to hear from you. For group emails, hit "Reply All" as a last resort, not a first.

10. Use the *New York Times* test. Would you be okay if your email were placed on the front page of tomorrow's edition? If not, you may need to rethink your message.

11. Use humor with caution. Without the normal social cues that come with communicating voice-

to-voice, "email" humor, especially sarcasm, can easily backfire.

12. Don't forward jokes, political or religious statements, or other items not relevant to work.

Finally, resist the temptation to fight via email. The more emotionally charged the message, the more personal you'll want to make your form of communication.

Example: Email is more personal than texting, a phone call is more personal than email, and face-to-face is more personal than a phone call. Just use your best judgment. But at the very least, don't put the other person's words in quotation marks, as in, *I didn't "make" you do anything*. It's only going to fan the flames.

But what about when you need or want a paper trail? You can always send the details you've discussed *after* the phone call. If you do decide to stick with email, let any caustic response on your part sit overnight in your drafts folder. By morning, you can read it with fresh eyes and decide if it even needs to be sent.

Overlooked Lesson in Cultural Competence

As a high school co-op student, my cousin Janis worked an office job at a large manufacturing plant. One day her boss asked her to get on the intercom and summon one of her fellow employees—a man she didn't know.

The man's name was Jesus. Only instead of pronouncing it "hey ZEUS," she called him Jesus! As in "Jesus Gonzales, please report to Human Resources."

Cue roaring laughter from the factory floor—including Jesus, and me every time I share this story. But here's the Ultimate Reminder I learned that day from Janis:

Don't forget how to laugh.

Life is hard enough—why make it harder? Be willing to laugh at and learn from your own innocent mistakes.

Bonus Article #1: 10 Tips for Leading New College Hires

When I moved across the country to start my master's program in counseling, I had no idea I would end up working with the millennial generation—and loving it.

That was 2001. As part of my program, I needed two semesters of internship. So with a year of coursework under my belt, I interviewed at my university's career services office and was hired to start my internship the following fall.

It was not easy. Despite my best efforts to connect with this age group, I found them giggly, unfocused, and all but out of reach. So much so that I wasn't sure I could take another semester.

But as I grew more confident with my counseling skills, I began to see so-called millennials differently. For all the talk of their entitlement, they also showed themselves to be endearingly grateful and optimistic.

Maybe too optimistic.

More than once I would get the heavy-hearted, wide-eyed question, "How do I handle it if I get two job offers at once?" I would share what I would do, then I would warmly remind them, "So far you haven't applied for either position."

How do you not fall in love with that? If you're a manager wanting to get the most from new college hires, here are my Ultimate Reminders for you:

1. **Don't call them millennials.** For one thing, people of this generation don't label themselves that way. For another, notice how often that word—and the tone behind it—are disparaging. So if you want more respect and cooperation from what's now the largest generation in the U.S. labor force, it's probably best to keep your use of the word "millennials" to a minimum.

2. **Trade managing for leading.** As Stephen Covey pointed out in *The 7 Habits of Highly Effective People,* we should manage things and lead people. To use the word "manage" with an entire class of

people is demeaning. It also implies falsely they are unreachable and unteachable.

3. **Be the boss, not the buddy.** Yes, I know I said this before. But sometimes in an effort to "connect" with young employees, we lower the bar when we should be raising it. As a young woman once said of a world youth leader, "He didn't try too hard to be like us. He made us want to be like him." If only every boss would post that sentiment to their wall and live by it.

4. **Take advantage of teachable moments.** Who among us hasn't made mistakes—especially when we were younger? I can also assure you this: Part of the reason new college grads don't grasp professional conduct is they didn't always see it modeled on campus. So it's up to us to teach them. Knowing this is part of our job makes the job easier. I can also assure you that new college hires are motivated to succeed—and they're eager to learn, especially if we treat them with warmth and respect.

5. **Let there be consequences.** Once when a graduating senior sauntered in late for a practice interview, my co-worker (the interviewer) told her with great cheer and gusto, "Good news, bad news! The good news: I'm still going to do your interview. The bad news: You didn't get the job!" His approach was fair—maybe more than fair. It's also a good example of combining consequences with a teachable moment.

6. **Model your expectations.** For example, if you want new hires to dress professionally, give them an example to follow.

7. **Give them a track to run on.** Show new hires how they can grow, and give them a path to do so. If they see it, they'll be more likely to stick around and give full effort along the way.

8. **Give employees at all levels a voice.** In the words of Max DePree, author of *Leadership Is an Art*, "Participative management is not democratic. Having a say differs from having a vote." Help

new employees appreciate this distinction. Who *doesn't* work harder when they know they are heard and respected?

9. **Take an appropriate interest in their lives.** Here's a simple question you can pose (in writing) to new hires of *any* age: "What are three things that would be helpful for me to know about you?" You might hear anything from "I have the cutest cat in the world" to "I lost my mom when I was ten and was raised by my granny."

   Breaking the ice with new hires not only shows a much-needed human side, it also helps bridge the gap between generations. As an example, one of my new hires once shared the statement about losing her mother at an early age and being raised by her grandmother. Two months later when her grandmother passed away unexpectedly, I knew right away this was no ordinary loss—and it allowed me to connect with even greater compassion.

Incidentally, when you ask new hires to divulge three things, be sure to reciprocate. Then in your next face-to-face meeting, start a conversation around what's on your lists.

10. **Don't ascribe the sins of one person to a whole generation.** You can do everything right as a manager, and you're still going to have employees who flake out, check out, or just don't work out. Keep in mind these tendencies might be generational, but as many or more are simply developmental.

According to Pew Research, the millennial workforce is 53.5 million strong. If we take time to nurture them, we can hold our heads high, knowing we're part of the solution—not just another adult grousing about "kids these days." And whether we realize it or not, we will also be nurturing our future co-workers, leaders, and friends.

Bonus Article #2: 9 Tips for New College Hires

First, unlike many of my middle-aged peers, I refuse to call you a millennial or a post-millennial. (You're welcome.) For one thing, these are labels and typically not very flattering ones. You'll be happy to hear I've asked my generation—specifically employers—to knock it off.

But because I care about you, I have some friendly reminders for how to succeed in the workplace.

These reminders come from a lifetime of working in the business world, serving as a university career counselor, interviewing countless employers, becoming a Certified Corporate Etiquette® and International Protocol Consultant, and speaking all over the United States on etiquette in the workplace.

So here goes:

1. **Earn thy credibility.** *You* know you're bright and capable. But does your boss or prospective boss? Be willing to demonstrate your credibility, not just through your words but through your work habits: coming in early, for example, and staying a bit late. Working hard while you're at work. Being able to take direction—and initiative.

2. **Check your work.** Part of earning credibility is showing that you listened and followed through. This means hand-checking your work before you hand it in.

3. **Be a problem-*solver*.** My mother taught me this. She said, "Don't go to your boss with a problem until you have a solution." Managers respect and appreciate employees who make their lives easier.

4. **Filter everything through "I am a professional."** I heard this from someone I interviewed long ago for an article on workplace etiquette. Let those four words ("I am a professional") affect your posture, your handshake, the texture of your voice, how you speak, and how you let others speak to you.

Let these four words affect your whole conduct. The point here isn't to be stiff or artificial. The point is to be yourself—your *best* self.

5. **Kick yourself harder in the behind than anyone else.** This does not mean "Beat yourself up." It just means to hold yourself to a higher standard than anyone else. Self-discipline is actually much easier and more rewarding than being "disciplined" by a boss, client, co-worker, or anyone else.

6. **Don't say "No problem" in response to something that was never understood to be a problem.** Here's an example: If you pull over in the middle of a snowstorm to help me change a tire and I thank you, you have a right to say "No problem"—because we both know it really *was* a problem. So saying "No problem" is actually reassuring.

   But if I thank Brittany for handing me a report that was due, and she says "No problem," that implies it *was* a problem—when really it was just part of her job. In a case like this, a better response to a thank-you is simply "You're welcome."

7. **Keep good company, on the job and off.** Right or wrong, we are known by the company we keep. Especially in the workplace, be careful not to align yourself with negative people. Be friendly, but recognize that not everyone gets to be your friend.

8. **Protect your brand.** Your brand is who you are when no one else is looking. Another word for brand could be *integrity.* It can take years to build your integrity and only one bad decision to destroy it. Online or offline, guard your integrity like the sacred thing it is.

9. **Have a life outside of work.** You know this, of course, but it helps to be reminded. As long as you live, keep growing, learning, and contributing. There is no faster cure for boredom and no better recipe for a life well lived.

"You've grown up with a steadily increasing access to everyone's everything, and the ability to transfer information at lightning speed. Confidentiality matters. Earn a reputation for never participating in office gossip."

—MY COUSIN JANIS'S ADVICE TO HER TWO YOUNG-ADULT DAUGHTERS

PART 3:

Stomping Out Drama

"You know you're a codependent if, when you are about to die, someone else's life flashes before you."

—OLD HUMOROUS SAYING

Set Boundaries for YOU

One night when my nephew Dylan was about five years old, he and his older siblings got together with the other neighborhood kids for "night games."

Dylan is the closest thing our family has to a minister. He is also a born athlete—so when the captains chose up teams and Dylan was picked last, he stormed off the field and shouted, "I don't have to take this sh*t!"

And he didn't. As adults, we don't willingly sign up for unacceptable treatment—but over time, it can creep in and start to appear normal. Examples:

- The friend in constant crisis mode, for whom no amount of your help will ever be enough.
- The co-worker who has forty-five minutes to drop by to tell you how busy he is.
- The client who misses deadlines and expects you to pick up the slack.

- The talented but hotheaded employee who wreaks havoc on office morale.
- Anyone who repeatedly breaks commitments to you, even minor ones.

You can't control these folks, and you will make yourself frustrated if you try. What you can do is decide what you will and won't put up with. That, in a nutshell, is what it means to set a boundary.

And while I'm not encouraging you to storm off the field and spew curse words, I am encouraging you to never apologize for having boundaries. Without them, you will suffer needlessly, cause suffering to those you love and work with, and live in the frustration of never reaching your full potential.

But *with* boundaries, you are practically unstoppable. Just ask Dylan, who's now in his twenties and living the dream. At his wedding reception, his older brother and best man proudly shared the night-games story.

Dylan's employer recently named him Outstanding Young Salesperson of the Year for North America.

More importantly, he is one of the kindest young men you could ever meet—and "I don't have to take this sh*t" is still a phrase worth remembering.

Boundaries, my friend. It all starts with boundaries.

What IS Drama?

Let's start with how it makes you feel. For example, if someone else's conduct or presence leaves you feeling drained, resentful, flustered, or depressed—even mildly so—you can bet you're experiencing drama.

At best, drama is a distortion of something good; something you would normally consider a virtue. Drama comes in all-too-many disguises. A few examples:

Virtue	**Drama equivalent**
Teamwork	Forming cliques
Hard work	Martyr-complex
High standards	Micromanagement
Friendship	Dependency
Intimacy	Intensity
Caring	Controlling

Drama occurs when someone tries to get their needs met in an unhealthy way—including at your expense. And while drama is often a cry for help, that doesn't mean it has to run or ruin your life. With the right tools and mindset, it won't.

10 Examples of Workplace Drama

1. The boss or co-worker who takes credit for your work
2. The self-proclaimed office spokesperson
3. The narcissist or know-it-all
4. The person who can't take feedback, no matter how justified and necessary
5. The boss who turns a blind eye
6. Anyone who gossips—or spills their guts
7. The person who always seems to be in crisis mode, even when there's no crisis
8. The employee who runs to the boss with a problem without first identifying a possible solution
9. Anyone who bullies, belittles, or betrays
10. The co-worker whose unspoken motto is "The rules don't apply to me."

What other scenarios would you add to this list?

The Weapons That Defeat Drama

A winner's mindset. Too often, we see drama as normal or inevitable. In truth, it is neither. Once you accept this, solutions become much simpler.

Self-confidence. Self-confidence does not mean cockiness, false bravado, or lone-ranger syndrome. It simply means trusting in your basic decency and worth, and trusting your ability to handle what life throws you.

Self-confidence is one of the best drama-repellants under the sun. Why? Because "drama" people look for easy targets. They want people they can manipulate. When you show them you're not interested—through your body language, words, and actions—they will either rise up to your level or take their drama somewhere else. Either way, you win.

Dispassion. Dispassion says, "I care about you, but I'm not responsible for you. I'll do my part, but I'm not going to own your baggage or negativity."

And no matter how much you want to help, don't become someone else's counselor. Just leave that to the professionals.

A willingness to be wildly uncomfortable. Defeating drama rarely happens in one hit-and-run encounter. And more often than not, it gets harder and rougher before it gets easier and smoother. Keep holding your ground—you don't need your boundaries to be liked. You just need them to be respected.

Courage. Courage allows us to admit our mistakes, honor our limitations, and deal with them constructively. All of these things help put drama in its place. And while you can't become someone else's counselor, there is no shame in seeking out counseling for yourself. It doesn't mean you're weak—it probably means you're strong. For what it's worth, today's technology allows you to receive therapy through your phone or laptop.*

---

* For an interesting article from the American Psychological Association, visit apa.org and search on "What you need to know before choosing online therapy."

Kindness. Though it may sound counterintuitive, being kind to someone who is being unkind (or just dramatic) can make drama melt. But don't be kind to change someone else. Be kind because it's the right thing to do. Be kind because tonight when your head hits the pillow, the only behavior you really have to be at peace with is your own.

The point is, don't let someone else's character diminish yours. Years ago when I was dealing with a drama person in my own life, a counselor I consulted gave me these lifesaving words, which I now pass on to you (say this inside your mind, not necessarily out loud to the other person):

*"If you're going to do drama,
you're going to do it without me."*

PART 4:

How to Make Your Mark

"Belong to people.
Accept pain as part of your life.
Know that you have made a difference."

—HAROLD KUSHNER,
When All You've Ever Wanted Isn't Enough

If You Want to Make a Difference

You don't have to move to Calcutta. You don't have to become a social worker. All you have to do is be an agent of hope. Right where you are.

How do you do that? You start with the little things, which over time become the big things.

In that spirit, here are 21 ways to be an agent of hope, particularly in the workplace. By the way, other words for hope include kindness and respect.

21 Ways to Be an Agent of Hope

1. Show up early.

2. Show up prepared.

3. Show up in a good mood.

4. Pitch in when you're expected to *and when you're not.*

5. Be the first to offer a smile.

6. Hold doors, including elevator doors.
7. Tone it down. No matter how much your co-workers love you, they don't want to hear you sing. Not even softly.
8. See the person in front of you as the most important person in the world.
9. Listen without interrupting.
10. Take hints the first time.
11. Pay meaningful compliments.
12. Don't hit people when they're down. Or up.
13. Celebrate others' successes. A few kind words and a high five go a long way.
14. When someone's telling a story, let them have the limelight.
15. Be quick to praise and slow to criticize. Most of us are doing the best we can.
16. Return what you've borrowed, without being asked.

17. Send a sincere, handwritten thank-you to one of your co-workers. Or your boss.

18. Let someone else cut in front of you at the copy machine or office microwave.

19. Clean up after yourself. Especially in the lunchroom.

20. Pick up the check.

21. Say please and thank you.

How will you be an agent of hope?

To Find Your Calling, Answer This Question

What is it you can't *not* do?

As an example, I can't *not* write. Often, I write to figure out what I'm thinking. I write because it's cheaper than therapy. It is almost as much a part of me as breathing.

But I also live to encourage other people, to make them laugh and inspire their best—in short, to remind them of their infinite worth. Writing and speaking are a means to this much higher end.

To live your calling, then, you need two things: (1) to use your gifts, the ones that often make you lose all track of time, and (2) to discern which *outcomes* make you feel most alive and contributing.

Your calling doesn't have to be lofty. It just has to be genuine. It just has to be yours. As the saying goes, "What comes from the heart *reaches* the heart."

Be a Gratitude Ninja

If you want to be happy and fulfilled, make gratitude a daily habit. Make it a way of life. I have never met a happy, generous soul who wasn't also extremely grateful—and good at showing it.

Gratitude does not mean settling. It's not about looking on the bright side or acquiescing. It is about recognizing every good thing you have and building on it.

If you're concerned that gratitude will make you wimpy, fear not. Gratitude will make you *more* powerful. For example, have you ever walked into a store, ready to buy a big-ticket item such as a bike or computer, only to have the sales staff ignore you?

When you live in conscious gratitude—including gratitude for your good mood—you're more likely to either ask a salesperson for help or simply walk away with your good mood intact. A state of gratitude allows you to let go and move forward more quickly.

5 Ways to Be a Gratitude Ninja

1. Create a simple, sustainable, daily ritual. For example, before you get out of bed in the morning, call to mind three things for which you are grateful.

2. Make a list of all the people who make your life better and easier—from your hairstylist to your CPA. Find a way to thank them in a way they would appreciate. For example, showing up on time, paying bills on time, and when the situation calls for it, tipping generously.

3. Say it while it counts. For example, if a co-worker goes out of his way for you, he would probably rather receive your gratitude now than a month from now.

4. Show *and* tell. For example, every week my virtual assistance team saves me countless hours of tasks I would find overwhelming. So when I write to thank them, I let them see the results of their efforts. *Example*: "Because of your work

on my behalf, I can enjoy my weekends." Let other people see the difference they make.

5. Keep it pure and simple. For example, don't spoil your praise by saying, "By the way, you forgot something" or "We're out of paper towels." Just let your praise go unblemished.

Last but not least, count your blessings. The more blessings you count, the more you find. Once you start counting, you will never run out of reasons to be thankful.

The natural response to gratitude is generosity. For the free article "Generosity on Any Income," visit UltimateReminders.com/free-downloads.

Six Words That Changed Everything

Have you ever found a few simple words so inspiring that they stayed with you forever? May the following story of hope and rejection—and hope fulfilled beyond expectation—lift your spirits just as someone lifted mine, long ago.

The Story of Jack Sanders

One night when I was in my twenties, a few Jaycee buddies and I were standing in a dark parking lot, shivering a little and saying goodbye. We had just wrapped up our monthly dinner meeting.

In case you're not familiar with it, Jaycee stands for "Junior Chamber of Commerce." The Grand Rapids, Michigan chapter, which was a big part of my life, stood as the second largest chapter in the country.

Jack Sanders was our chapter president: a good family man, the kind of leader who couldn't be unkind if he tried. He was also the spitting image of comedian Jon Lovitz—a trait that only endeared him to us all the more.

So back to the dark parking lot. A few of us, including Jack, were talking and laughing about nothing in particular. Finally, I turned toward my car. About ten steps later, Jack called out, "Gina!" I turned to see what he wanted.

He smiled and said, "Don't let anyone steal your dreams."

When someone you admire and look up to hands you a vote of confidence, you treasure it. That night I wrote "Don't let anyone steal your dreams" on my quote board, with Jack's name underneath. It's still there, though I haven't seen Jack in over twenty years.

Fast Forward to the Other Day

I'm in my office, rummaging through a box of long-forgotten cards and letters. I come across a couple of brief, handwritten thank-you notes from Jack—and a brief (typewritten) rejection letter from Iowa; specifically, the University of Iowa Graduate Department of English. Even now, as I type those words, I stop a moment and smile.

There's no way I could have known in 1997 how much unimaginable good would come from that one closed door.

All I knew was this: I was disappointed, hurt, and embarrassed. I even cried a little. It wasn't so much that I wanted to *go* to Iowa. But I wanted the option. I wanted the validation of being accepted. It took awhile to let it go.

Life went on, Iowa faded from memory, and other lessons appeared in Technicolor.

From Rejection to Recommendation

There simply isn't room here to recount all the gifts that the Iowa rejection made possible—including a move to San Diego, a master's degree in counseling, a six-year teaching stint at my alma mater, and a life where I get paid to be a listening ear and a voice of encouragement.

There is, however, one more story that brings it all full circle.

A few years ago, one of my star students at the University of San Diego (USD) came to me with a heavy heart. She was standing at a difficult crossroads and needed help discerning her options.

So one night at her request, the two of us stayed after class to talk. We stayed for hours. It turns out she was applying to doctoral programs, and she wondered if I would write her a letter of recommendation.

"Of course," I said. "By the way, where are you applying?"

"University of Iowa."

Insert lump in throat.

I wrote Cindy the best letter I could, and proudly put it on USD letterhead.

Cindy gained acceptance into a program that was more selective by far than the one I had applied to. (And yes, I *did* just end that sentence with a preposition. Eat your heart out, Hawkeyes.)

Today my former student is thriving in Iowa City. I smile to think my earlier rejection helped pave the way to her acceptance. Meanwhile, I still get to be a writer. And I get to be me, (with all due respect) not some stuffy cartoon version of myself.

Don't let anyone steal your dreams.

Least of all, the University of Iowa or the University of Anywhere. The world needs what you're itching to offer. If you want to write, write. If you want to paint, paint. Why wait for permission or perfection?

And if you do get a rejection letter (assuming it isn't toxic), tuck it away somewhere. Years from now, it will probably resurface. *Let it.* Let it remind you of who you are today and just how far you've come.

"Write to your heart's content, and never stop writing. Do not let anyone steal your dreams or enthusiasm, let alone your love for writing. Some will try. You must let them go and move forward. Some will write far better than you—or be more commercially successful. But the good writers who are also good people will always encourage and celebrate your writing. Again, if they don't, you have to let them go."

—WHAT I TOLD THE YOUNG ASPIRING WRITER WHO ASKED FOR MY ADVICE

Learning to Say Goodbye

No matter how much you love your current career, there may come a time when you're called to leave it behind. Why? Because there's something even better waiting for you. You'll know it in your bones, even if you can't quite put it into words.

The enemy of the best isn't something bad.
The enemy of the best is something good.

In my case, I was up for a promotion and a rather juicy raise at the university where I worked. But my priorities were shifting.

For one thing, I had just lost my childhood best friend, unexpectedly, and the loss felt primal. Susie and I had known each other since age four. I still remember her tiger costume from the preschool Halloween party.

Fast forward to adulthood. Have you ever watched a friend make poor choices you were helpless to do anything about? As we say in counseling,

Susie was beyond my therapeutic reach. And for a while after she died, so was I.

What kept me going, and some days still does, is a belief that I could make her proud—and I would. Along with this life-altering loss came the realization that I was being called to do something more. And whatever it was, I needed to get on with it.

So after several months of intense soul-searching and a well-timed pep talk from my dad, I scheduled a meeting with my boss, and together we came up with the best possible transition plan.

Meanwhile, from my home office in Grand Rapids, I was mentally making my way back to San Diego.

I tell you all of this to help you make sense of your own transitions, because you're going to be going through them for the rest of your life. And it takes more than a counseling degree to get through them successfully.

Here's a passage from a book I read before entering grad school, and one I've read a couple of times since. From William Bridges' book *The Way of Transition*:

> Transition does not require that you reject or deny the importance of your old life, just that you let go of it. Far from rejecting it, you are likely to do better with the ending if you honor the old life for all that it did for you. It got you this far. It brought you everything you have. But now—although it may be some time before you are comfortable actually doing so—it is time for you to let go of it. Your old life is over. No matter how much you would like to continue it or rescue it or fix it, it's time to let it go.[1]

All-righty. Not exactly brought to you by Hallmark. As this passage implies, growth doesn't tickle. But you didn't come this far so you could be comfortable. You came this far so you could grow and never stop growing. So you could be inspired and *be an inspiration.*

Toward that end, would you like to know the secret to a graceful goodbye?

---

[1] William Bridges, *The Way of Transition,* p. 16 (2001, Perseus Publishing, Cambridge, MA)

Leave at your peak,
and leave on good terms.

My parents taught me this, especially that last part. Don't just serve somebody papers. Go out of your way to show respect for your employer, especially your boss.

Thanks in no small part to my father's prodding, I did. My graceful ending with Grand Valley State University allowed me to continue our professional relationship, long after I had left. More than ten years later, I'm proud to say I'm still friends with several of my former GVSU co-workers.

Through his example and guidance, my father taught me an important lesson: How you finish is how you'll be remembered.

How would you like to be remembered?

EPILOGUE:

Make Your Life a Work of Art

Scott Adams, the cartoonist who gave us *Dilbert*, said this: "Creativity is allowing yourself to make mistakes. Art is knowing which ones to keep."

Let's wrap up with the true story of a young man named Jimmy, who made all kinds of mistakes—but found a few he could keep.

The summer he turned sixteen, Jimmy went to work full time in the restaurant business. And by the end of that summer, he was hooked.

He decided he would be the first in his family to go to college. But his friends and neighbors scoffed, and the university where he applied turned him down.

So he applied to a two-year college. And once more, he was rejected. Finally, someone at this two-year institution went to bat for him with the college president.

As the three men sat in the president's office, the president looked at Jimmy's high school transcript and gravely shook his head.

Sensing this was his only hope, Jimmy blurted out, "Why don't you give me a chance to prove myself?"

The president looked at the professor. Finally he looked at Jimmy and said, "All right, young man. Show us what you can do. You've got three months to make the grade."

And he did. No way was Jimmy returning to his old neighborhood, a failure and a laughingstock.

Dissolve, as they say in film, to a few years later. Jimmy did well enough in school that he graduated with a four-year degree in hotel-restaurant management—from the university where he had originally applied.

And while he was in school, he fell in love. On his wedding day, one of the wedding guests actually said, "They'll never last." Wasn't me.

Over the next six years, Jimmy went through five jobs. The fifth one was the worst. During dinner at the restaurant where he worked, on his one night off, the boss marched up to his table and ripped him to shreds—told him everything that was wrong with him, in front of his wife and their mortified friends.

Meanwhile, Jimmy's doctor is telling him, "You are *exactly* the kind of person who will have a heart attack before age forty."

Ouch. By now you're probably thinking, "I'm glad I'm not *that* guy." I don't blame you.

But that's not the end of the story. Because the young man who couldn't keep a job? He was meant to create jobs. And in following his dream to get into the pizza business, he created hundreds of jobs in a small town that needed them.

Long before he became successful, Jimmy went out of his way to help others. And when he became successful, he went back to that two-year college to name a scholarship for the president who opened a door, when his whole future hung in the balance.

How do you make your life a work of art? You take those things that seem like your worst setbacks and you turn them into rocket fuel. You let them propel you upward and onward. You don't let anyone steal your soul or diminish your dreams. You find creative, meaningful ways to give back—or pay it forward.

Think of someone who believed in you, maybe before you believed in yourself. Tonight before your head hits the pillow, think about how you can thank that person one more time.

What about our man Jimmy, who was headed for a heart attack before age forty? By the grace of God, he has *never* had a heart attack—and today he's eighty-three. *Eighty-three.*

Every June I have the privilege of calling this man to say, "Happy Father's Day, Dad. You made it."

My dad, with everything he's lived through, made it further than anyone ever dreamed he would. And you, with everything you've got going for you and everything you've lived through, can go further than anyone dreamed *you* would—and inspire others in ways you don't even realize. You might even inspire the person in the mirror.

My dad doesn't know I'm telling you all this. I'm not even sure how much he knows about this book. But when I call to tell him how I wrote all hours of the day and night, not as a chore but as a chance to touch your life, he'll say to me what he always does:

"Okay, well, here's your mother!"

Which reminds me. To that wedding guest who said my parents would never last? *Ha*! Fifty-nine years, three sons and a daughter, two daughters-in-law, six grandkids, three with spouses, two gorgeous great-grandbabies named Maddie and Leo, and more where that came from.

As my mother likes to say, "We may not have it all together. But together we have it all." And as my father likes to say, *"Together, we're stronger than garlic."*

I'm asking you to be stronger than garlic. To be

stronger than anything life throws at you. Let every setback propel you forward. Give back to those who help you, and maybe even to those who hurt you—not to change them, but so they don't change you.

Finally, to paraphrase from my book *Ultimate Reminders for Everyday Life*:

Your life matters.
Make it a brilliant, priceless work of art.

Acknowledgments

Heartfelt thanks to Jared Kuritz of STRATEGIES Literary Public Relations, who helped make this book possible, compelling, and fun—and to Gwyn Snider of GKS Creative, for endless creativity and patience.

I also wish to thank the following people and their respective firms for their influence on my work:

Mary Altbaum, Editor/Proofreader

Bonnie B | Busy as a B San Diego

Mandi Holmes | She Can Coterie

Emily Lewis & Lea Alcantara | Bright Umbrella

Craig Valentine MBA, 1999 World Champion of Public Speaking

To the readers of my Monday-Morning Pep Talk, who lent their insights to this work, thank you! I love starting my week with you. Not yet a subscriber? It's free! **To sign up, text PEPTALK to 66866.**

Finally, my highest thanks and praise to the Triune God. Apart from Him, I can do nothing (John 15:5).

How to Reach Us

For more information on how Gina DeLapa can help your organization thrive, please visit UltimateReminders.com. A sneak peek at what you will find:

- **A contact form** so you can get in touch*
- **Speaking clips** to help you determine how Gina can add life to your next event
- The **Ultimate Reminders® book series** which make wonderful, well-received gifts
- **Online opportunities** to fuel your personal and professional growth
- **Monday-Morning Pep Talk**, Gina's free dose of inspiration to help you start each week feeling energized, empowered, and unstoppable. To sign up now, text PEPTALK to 66866.

* If you just can't wait, simply send an email to info@ultimatereminders.com and someone will respond as quickly as possible. We look forward to hearing from you!

About the Author

Gina DeLapa, America's Ultimate Reminders® Coach, is all about helping you **Live life more fulfilled.**™

As a professional speaker, former university career counselor, and adjunct faculty member, Gina not only gives audiences the tools and inspiration they need to succeed, she engages them with humor, candor, and powerful stories that touch and transform.

A few of her most requested speaking topics:

- Recharged and Refreshed: Taking Better Care of YOU, Guilt-Free
- Making a Meaningful Difference at Work
- Workplace Etiquette for New-College Hires

Gina received certification as a Corporate Etiquette and International Protocol Consultant by the prestigious Protocol School of Washington®. She has taught and inspired audiences from Orange County to Wall Street. Why not let her add life to your next event?

For speaking and all other inquiries, please visit UltimateReminders.com/contact. You may also send your request to info@ultimatereminders.com.

CPSIA information can be obtained
at www.ICGtesting.com
Printed in the USA
FSHW02n0816230518
48555FS

9 780989 629195